Space Objects: Comets, Asteroids, and Meteors

Steve Parker

rosen publishing's
rosen
central

New York

New Hanover County Public Library
201 Chestnut Street
Wilmington, North Carolina 28401

Published in 2008 by The Rosen Publishing Group, Inc.
29 East 21st Street, New York, NY 10010

First Edition

Editor: Nicola Edwards
Designer: Tim Mayer
Consultant: Ian Graham

The right of Steve Parker to be identified as the author of this work has been asserted by him in accordance
with the Copyright, Designs, and Patents Act, 1988.

Cover photograph: A meteor shower, taken over many minutes. The photograph shows ordinary stars moving
as slightly curved streaks.

Photo credits: Michael Abbey/SPL: 35; Julian Baum/New Scientist/SPL: 17; Bettmann/Corbis: 14; Jonathan
Blair/Corbis: 34; Chris Butler/SPL: 18; Peter Casolino/Sygma/Corbis: 5; Dennis di Cicco/SPL: 12;
Dreamworks/Paramount/The Kobal Collection: 24; ESA: 9; ESA/AOES Medialab: 8; Dr Fred Espenak/SPL: front
cover, 32; Mark Garlick/SPL: 26; A. Gragera/Latin Stock/SPL: 43; Victor Habbick Visions/SPL: 33; Hayabusa: 41;
John Hopkins University Applied Physics Lab/Southwest Research Institute: 27; John Hopkins University
Applied Physics Lab/SPL: 23; JPL/Cal-Tech/NASA: 7; JPL/UMD/NASA: 40; © Keck Observatory: 21; Mehau
Kulyk/SPL: 1,31; Claus Lunau/Foci/Bonnier Publications/SPL: 11; Gianni Dagli Orti/Corbis: 13; NASA: 15, 16, 29,
42; NASA/ESA/STSCI/B.Zellner; GSU/SPL: 20; NASA/SPL: 10, 19, 22, 37; Pekka Parviainen/SPL: 28;
Picturepoint/Topfoto: 45; Roger Ressmeyer/Corbis: 4, 38; Reuters/Corbis: 30; D. Roddy, CUS Geological Survey,
Lunar & Planetary Institute: 36; Dennis Scott/Corbis: 25; WIYN/NOAO/AURA/NSF/epa/Corbis: 6; Frank Zullo/SPL:
39.

Manufactured in China

Contents

Smaller Objects in Space

Most of the objects we see in the night sky are huge. Twinkling stars look tiny because they are so far away. But some are thousands of times bigger than our nearest star, the Sun. Much closer to home than the stars are smaller objects in space. They may be relatively tiny. But they provide fascinating information about the Sun, Earth, and the other planets, as well as how all these objects began—and how they might end.

The Solar System

The Sun is a *star*—a massive object in space that gives off energy, mainly light and heat. Earth is a planet—a relatively large object that goes around, or orbits, a star. In Earth's case, the star is the Sun. A moon (such as Earth's Moon) is an object that orbits a planet. Our neighboring planet Mars has two moons, but the huge planet Jupiter has more than 60. The Sun, all of its planets, and all of their moons form most of the Solar System.

Types of smaller objects

Apart from the Sun, planets, and their moons, there are other kinds of objects in the Solar System. Three of these are comets, asteroids, and meteoroids.

The Galileo *space probe took this close-up photograph of the asteroid Ida in 1993.*

Comets are small lumps of mixed dust, frozen "ice," and other small chunks that may follow very long, lop-sided orbits around the Sun. They come close to the Sun, then head out into the depths of the Solar System or beyond, before heading back to the Sun again. Other comets pass by the Sun once, never to return.

Asteroids are rocky lumps, smaller than planets that go around the Sun. Sometimes they are called "minor planets" or "planetoids." Most asteroids orbit in the wide gap between the planets Mars and Jupiter.

Meteoroids burn up near Earth as "shooting stars."

Meteoroids are little pieces of rock and other substances that are smaller than asteroids. Most are tinier than grains of sand or bits of dust. Some meteoroids orbit the Sun, but others whizz through space on random paths through the Solar System.

In 2006, a world gathering of space experts decided that comets, asteroids, meteoroids, and similar objects orbiting the Sun, that were not planets or moons, should all be known by the general name of Small Solar System Bodies, SSSBs, or "S3Bs."

SPACE DATA

Here are some sizes of space objects to compare:

	Diameter (distance across)
Sun (a star)	863,040 mi. (1,392,000 km)
Jupiter (the biggest planet)	88,600 mi. (142,900 km)
Earth	7,909 mi. (12,756 km)
Mercury (the smallest planet)	3,026 mi. (4,880 km)
Moon (Earth's Moon)	2,158 mi. (3,480 km)
Pallas (biggest asteroid)	335 mi. (540 km)
Halley's Comet (its central core or nucleus)	9 mi. (15 km)
Meteoroids	Vary greatly but usually yards to minute fractions of an inch

Comet Heads and Tails

The name of this comet, C/2001 Q4 (NEAT), shows it was discovered in the year 2001 by the Near-Earth Asteroid Tracking organization, NEAT.

Space Facts

A comet's coma and tails can be truly vast.

● Most comas are around 62,000 miles (100,000 kilometers) across.

● Some comas are more than 930,000 miles (1.5 million kilometers) across, which is bigger than the Sun.

● Some tails are 93 million miles (150 million kilometers) long—the same distance as from Earth to the Sun.

● Two of the longest tails—350 million mi. (570 million km)—belonged to the very bright Comet Hyakutake in 1996.

Comets are mysterious space objects that shine in the night sky, with a front end or head, and a long, streaklike, glowing tail. Some are unexpected and appear from nowhere. Others come back time and time again after gaps of years. We can predict their appearance to within days or even hours.

What do comets look like?

A typical comet has a small, solid lump in its head, called its *nucleus* (see page 8). When we view a comet from Earth, the nucleus is much too small to see. What we see are other parts of a comet. These are its coma and its tail. In fact, there are usually two tails, one made from dust and one of gas.

The comet's coma

Earth has a layer of air around it, called the *atmosphere*. A comet has an atmosphere, too, although this is much thinner and more wispy than Earth's, and it extends much farther out into space. A comet's atmosphere is called the *coma* and it surrounds the nucleus as a glow. It is made of dust and gases given off by the nucleus as this is heated by the Sun.

This drawing shows how the center or nucleus of Comet Wild 2 might have looked, as the Stardust *space probe passed in January 2004.*

The Sun sends out powerful amounts of ray and wave energy, or radiation, including light rays and heat (infrared) waves. The Sun also sends out streams of particles called the *solar wind*. Both the radiation and solar wind leave the Sun in all directions, streaming out into deep space.

Two tails

The radiation and particles from the Sun "blow" the comet's thin, flimsy coma into one or more tails that spread out from the head. The tails do not trail behind the comet as it zooms along. They always point away from the Sun.

One type of tail is the dust tail. This may be slightly curved, due to the comet's fast movement through space. The other type of tail is the gas tail. This is usually straight, because the gas is lighter and blown more strongly by the Sun. The dust tail shines, because its bits of dust reflect, or bounce back, sunlight. The gas tail glows, because the gas particles in it themselves give out light.

Inside a Comet

Ideas about comets have changed greatly over the years. In particular, long-traveling spacecraft have made exciting discoveries during the past few years. These finds have helped to answer the mystery of what is inside a comet and show how it changes as it travels closer to the Sun and then away again.

Changing ideas

In the middle of a comet's head is its nucleus—a small, very dark lump. Most comet nuclei are less than 31 miles (50 kilometers) across. An early scientific suggestion was that the nucleus of a comet was a "gravel bank" of bits of stones like small pebbles, contained in a layer of ice. In 1950, the U.S. astronomer, Fred Whipple, suggested the famous "dirty snowball" idea. This described the nucleus as small bits of dust and rocky debris mixed into a huge lump of ice. The ice was not simply frozen water but other frozen substances, too, like methane, carbon dioxide, and ammonia (which are gases here on Earth).

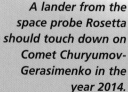

Space Facts

Comet nuclei

● Comet nuclei vary greatly in size. Comet Hale-Bopp's nucleus is 25 mi. (40 km) across, and Comet Hyakutake's nucleus is 1.25 mi. (2 km) across.

● Most comet nuclei are around 0.6–31 mi. (1–50 km) across.

A lander from the space probe Rosetta should touch down on Comet Churyumov-Gerasimenko in the year 2014.

In 2005, the spacecraft *Deep Impact* sent a small "impactor" to smash into the surface of the nucleus of Comet Tempel 1. The results showed that the nucleus contained less ice than previously thought, and more dust and rocky particles. So the description of a comet nucleus has changed from a "dirty snowball," with more ice than dust, to an "icy dirtball," with more rocky debris and dust than ice.

Switched on

A comet does not always have its coma and tails. In deep space, it is just the nucleus—a small, dark lump like a blob of road tar. It only starts to form its coma and tails when it comes close enough to the warmth of the Sun to heat up and "switch on." This usually happens when the nucleus enters an area of the Solar System that is closer to the Sun than Jupiter. Then the surface of the nucleus begins to warm up. Cracks appear and jets of gas blast out, carrying dust and chunks of rock. The comet grows its coma, looking like a fuzzy star. Then its tails form and grow longer as the comet nears the Sun.

After the comet curves around the Sun, it gradually becomes cooler as it travels away. Its tails shorten, its coma fades, and the surface of its nucleus, now too cold to spurt out dust and gas, becomes calm and still. Finally, the comet "switches off" as it heads away to the cold darkness of deep space.

The Giotto probe was launched in July 1985 and passed within 370 miles (600 kilometers) of Halley's Comet in March 1986.

How do we know?

Halley's Comet

During Halley's Comet's last visit in 1986, the *Giotto* spacecraft flew past and sent back close-up pictures of its almost black nucleus sending out jets of gas and spurts of dust. Other craft that have visited Halley's Comet include *Vegas 1* and *2*, and *Sakigake* and *Suisei*.

Comets' Journeys

Some comets are seen only once, and then disappear into deep space. Others return every so often, coming around on the same familiar pathway. Astronomers (experts on objects and events in space) can follow a comet's movements to find out where it has been, as well as where it is heading and how long it will take to get there.

Regular and irregular visitors

Comets that appear only once and then travel away on a nonreturn path are known as single-pass, single-apparition, or *nonperiodic comets*. They may simply zoom through space forever, or perhaps smash into another space object such as a planet.

Comet Encke was discovered by Jean Louis Pons, but named after Johann Franz Encke, who worked out its orbit time.

Comets that return regularly to loop around, or orbit, the Sun are known as *periodic comets*. Most are in very long, elliptical (oval) paths or orbits, with the Sun within one end of the orbit, pulling the comet with its immense gravity. The final fates of comets vary. Some crash into planets, moons, asteroids, or the Sun itself. Others break up into small fragments or gradually burn away after several passes around the Sun.

The long and the short

Short-period comets complete one orbit in less than 200 years. Long-period comets take more than 200 years for an orbit. This means that long-period comets discovered within the past 200 years have yet to return. But astronomers can work out their orbital time, or period, from the comet's speed and curved pathway.

SPACE DATA

Comets vary in the time they take to complete one orbit:

Comet Encke	3 years 4 months (one of the shortest)
Comet Biela	6 years 7 months
Comet Tempel-Tuttle	33 years
Halley's Comet	76 years
Comet Hale-Bopp	2,380 years
Comet West	500,000 years

Where do comets orbit?

The planets of the Solar System orbit the Sun in the same plane, or level, as though they are spread out on a circular table top. Comets are found not just in this plane. They orbit the Sun at many different angles—that is, above and below the "table top."

Most short-period comets probably orbit from near the Sun out to the Kuiper Belt. This is a zone of space objects beyond the planet Neptune (see page 26). The orbits of most long-period comets probably extend much farther, into the Oort Cloud. This is a vast ball-like "shell" of objects at the edge of the Solar System, thousands of times more distant than the planets farthest from the Sun. The Oort Cloud may be the home of trillions of "sleeping" comets. Every now and then, one is pulled inward and begins its immense journey into the Solar System.

(see page 26)

Comets may loop around the Sun, "graze" past it, or head out into deep space (lower left).

Comets in History

Comets have fascinated people since ancient times. They appeared as if from nowhere, shining in the night sky and following strange paths, unlike the Moon and stars. No wonder they were linked with gods and spirits—usually as bringers of evil.

Space Facts

Comet Biela

● Comet Biela was one of the first comets to be shown as periodic—a regular visitor. It was first seen in 1772 and regularly every 6.6 years from then.

● During its 1846 passage, it seemed to break into two. These pieces were seen separately in 1852 but never since then.

Hairy stars

Aristotle of Ancient Greece helped to invent the word "comet." It comes from a Greek term "komet" meaning "hair," and Aristotle referred to comets as "stars with hair." For centuries, comets, like eclipses, were thought to be mysterious chariots of the gods, perhaps visiting Earth to take revenge, or maybe aliens from another world, or evil spirits. Some people offered gifts and carried out sacrifices of animals and people, to appease the comet-god so that it would go away—which it always did.

In the air or up in space?

Early astronomers thought that comets were, like clouds, within Earth's layer of air, the atmosphere. But the studies of the Danish scientist, Tycho Brahe, in the 1500s and the English astronomer, Edmund Halley, in the late 1600s and early 1700s, showed that they were far above Earth, in space like the Moon, Sun, and stars. Halley was excited by the so-called Great Comet of 1680, one of the brightest ever. He had the new idea that each comet sighting, as recorded by astronomers for centuries, might not always be a "new" comet. It could be an "old" one coming back at regular intervals.

Comet Kohoutek, named after the Czech astronomer, Lubos Kohoutek, went past Earth in 1973—and will come back in 75,000 years.

Halley's Comet

Edmund Halley worked out that sightings in 1531, 1607, and 1682 could all be the same comet. He predicted it would return in 1758 after another gap of 76 years. He was right and the comet was named after him. (He never saw it, since he died 16 years earlier.) Working backward into history, astronomers found that Halley's Comet has been sighted for more than 2,200 years. It is shown in the background of the Bayeux Tapestry, which records William the Conqueror's invasion of England under King Harold, in 1066.

In 1066, Halley's Comet was called a "comet-star" and believed to bring bad luck—which it did to King Harold.

How do we know?

Discovering comets

As we build improved telescopes and launch more technically advanced spacecraft, hundreds of new comets are now being discovered every year. The *SOHO* satellite (*SOlar and Heliospheric Observatory*) orbits the Sun about 930,000 miles (1.5 million kilometers) away from Earth. Its main task is to study the Sun, but since its launch in 1995, it has discovered over 1,000 comets.

Naming Comets

For many years after the naming of Halley's Comet, comets were named after people—usually their discoverers. But as more are identified, sometimes dozens in a week, this method has become very difficult. So a proper scientific naming system runs alongside the "everyday" one.

An everlasting name

Centuries ago, comets were named after the year in which they appeared, and also some feature of their visit, such as the September Comet of 1882 or the Daylight Comet of January 1910 (so called because of its immense brightness). The tradition also grew of naming a comet after the person who first discovered it or observed its orbit, if this person was known. Halley's Comet was the first to have a widespread "human name," from about 1759.

The tradition for naming a comet after the person who first spotted it means that comets are a great way for amateur astronomers to make an "everlasting" name for themselves. It is very difficult even for professional astronomers to predict when and where a comet will appear. So hobbyist stargazers have a chance of spotting a comet before the professionals discover it.

Edmund Halley (1656–1742) was British Astronomer Royal from 1720 until his death.

Space facts

Comet Tuttle-Giacobini-Kresak was discovered three times:

● By Horace Tuttle in 1858.

● By Michel Giacobini in 1907.

● By Lubor Kresak in 1951.

● This comet is one of the "Jupiter family," meaning that its farthest point from the Sun is near the planet Jupiter.

● It flares up brightly now and then. The last major flare was in 1973.

Space Facts

Orbiting Jupiter

● In March 1993, Shoemaker and Levy discovered a new comet, provisionally named Shoemaker-Levy 9.

● This was the first comet discovered that was not orbiting the Sun. It was going around the planet Jupiter.

● Also, it was not a single lump or nucleus, but had broken into 20-plus pieces or fragments, the largest being about 1.25 mi. (2 km) across.

● During mid-July 1994, the fragments plunged into Jupiter at speeds of up to 37 miles (60 kilometers) per second.

● The collisions caused massive, stormlike disturbances that could still be seen on Jupiter months later.

Usually, up to three names are allowed for this "unofficial" system. If the same person or people discover several comets, then these are given numbers. The Shoemaker-Levy comets (see panel) were found by Carolyn Shoemaker and David Levy, using a wide-viewing telescope at the Palomar Observatory California. (Levy has a double honor—an asteroid is also named after him.)

Discovered by machine

Some comets are discovered by huge teams of astronomers with very specialist equipment. The equipment sometimes gets mentioned in the naming. Comet IRAS-Araki-Alcock was found by the *IRAS* satellite and separately by Genichi Araki and George Alcock.

Alongside this "unofficial" system, which is easy for most people to understand, astronomers also have an official number-and-letter system for naming comets. This shows the order of their discovery compared to other comets, and tracks the year of each visit. In this system, Halley's Comet is known as 1P/Halley (P = Periodic) and the code for its last appearance in 1986 is 1P/1986III.

Dark patches near the bottom of Jupiter show where pieces of Comet Shoemaker-Levy 9 plunged into its swirling gases.

How Asteroids were Formed

Asteroids are rocky lumps less than 620 miles (1,000 kilometers) across that, like the planets, whirl around the Sun. They were formed at the same time as the rest of the Solar System. Most asteroids are found in a zone called the Asteroid Belt or Main Belt. This occupies the large gap between the last of the small inner planets, Mars, and the first of the giant outer planets, Jupiter.

Origin of asteroids

The whole Solar System probably formed about 4,600 million years ago. A vast cloud of gas and dust floating in space, called a *nebula*, gradually started to clump together into larger lumps. This clumping may have been caused by the explosion of a nearby star, known as a *supernova*. Attracted to each other by the force called gravity, the lumps formed a tighter ball shape that began to whirl around like a spinning top.

NGC 2423

NGC 2438

M47

M46

Pallas

This telescope view shows the largest asteroid, Pallas, among groups of stars indicated by the M (Messier) and NGC (New General Catalogue) code numbers.

How do we know?
Filling the gap

In 1800, a group of astronomers called the "Celestial Police" started searching for a missing planet. From the distances of the planets known then, there seemed to be a suspiciously empty "gap" between Mars and Jupiter. In 1801, the Italian astronomer, Giuseppe Piazzi, discovered the "dwarf planet" Ceres in the gap—but almost by accident, since he was not a member of the "police." However, over the following few years, the "police" found three asteroids—Pallas, Vesta, and Juno.

Artists' views of the Main Belt often show the asteroids (smaller lumps) as close together, whereas really they are huge distances apart.

The great mass at the center of the nebula came together to form the Sun. Smaller clumps formed the planets, including rocky ones like Earth and Mars, and gas giants, such as Jupiter and Saturn. Even smaller rocky bits and pieces became the asteroids. They collected in the gap between Mars and Jupiter, probably pulled there by Jupiter's great gravity. So asteroids are "leftovers" from the formation of the Solar System, too small to become proper planets. Sometimes they are called minor planets or *planetoids*.

The effect of being small

Because of their small size, most asteroids did not have enough gravity to form into ball-like shapes or spheres as they spun around. Many are shaped like lumpy potatoes. Unlike the planets of the Solar System, asteroids cannot hold a layer of gases or atmosphere around them.

Three belts

The Main Belt is made up of three belts, called the Inner, Middle, and Outer Belts. There are gaps between these known as Kirkwood Gaps. Fewer asteroids orbit in the Kirkwood Gaps, due to the balance between the gravities of the Sun and Jupiter.

Space Facts

The Main Belt

- The Main Belt contains more than nine-tenths of all known asteroids.

- The Belt begins at about 186 million mi. (300 million km) from the Sun. (The orbit of Mars averages 141 million mi. or 228 million km from the Sun.)

- The Belt fades by 310 million mi. (500 million km) from the Sun. (The orbit of Jupiter averages 483 million mi. or 779 million km from the Sun.)

Asteroids Big and Small

The sizes of asteroids range from over 310 miles (500 kilometers) to tens of yards across. There are very few asteroids at the larger end of the scale, but as the sizes decrease, the number of asteroids increases. Scientists have discovered what asteroids are made of, as well as what they look like.

Asteroid size and mass

Around 220 asteroids are larger than 62 miles (100 kilometers) across. Pallas is the largest asteroid, measuring about 335 miles (540 kilometers) in length. The next largest is Vesta, which is only slightly smaller than Pallas. Vesta has a light-colored surface and is the brightest asteroid when viewed from Earth.

The mass of an object is the amount of matter or substance in it. On Earth we measure it as weight. The total mass of all the known asteroids is less than 3.3 billion billion tons. This is tiny for space objects—only 1/25th of the mass of the Moon.

Many asteroids have bowl-like craters where they have bumped into each other.

SPACE DATA

The biggest asteroids are:

	Length or diameter
Pallas	335 mi. (540 km)
Vesta	329 mi. (530 km)
Hygiea	267 mi. (430 km)
Interamnia	211 mi. (340 km)
Davida	201 mi. (325 km)

What are asteroids made of?

Unlike the glowing gas tail of a comet (see page 7), asteroids do not give off their own light. Like the planets and moons, they shine by bouncing back or reflecting sunlight. Studies of the light reflected by asteroids, as well as the evidence collected by flybys and visits by spacecraft, have revealed that asteroids are mostly rock and/or metal. Some asteroids are rich in carbonaceous (carbon-based) rock. Some contain more silicaceous (silicon-based) rock such as quartz—familiar on Earth as sand grains. The M-type asteroids are mainly metals, especially iron or iron-nickel.

Gaspra was the first asteroid to be visited by a space probe, Galileo, in 1991.

Most asteroids have surfaces pockmarked with gouges, scars, and circular, bowl-like shapes called *craters*. These marks have been made by past collisions, mostly with other asteroids and meteoroids. Since an asteroid has no atmosphere, there is no weathering or wearing down of the surface as there is on Earth, so the marks stay for huge spans of time. The surface appearance will only change as a result of further collisions.

Space Facts

Discovering asteroids

● Many thousands of asteroids have been discovered and given names and numbers. For example, the biggest asteroid, Pallas, is known as 2 Pallas, and Eros is known as 433 Eros.

● There could be two million asteroids that are half a mile across or larger.

● The total number of asteroids in the Main Belt is probably many millions.

Asteroids Near and Far

Asteroids take several years to orbit the Sun—longer than their neighboring planet nearer the Sun, Mars, but shorter than the next planet out, Jupiter. Asteroids also spin around, like the planets. Apart from the Main Belt asteroids, there are asteroids elsewhere in the Solar System. Many of these are close to other planets, probably held there by each planet's pull of gravity balanced with the Sun's gravity.

A computer-colored map of Vesta shows its highest mountains as white, then going lower to red, yellow, green, and blue, to the deepest valleys as black.

Asteroid movements

Most asteroids in the Main Belt take between three and six years to orbit the Sun. For example, Vesta goes around once in about 3 years and 7 months. This time is one "year" for Vesta, so it is more than three-and-a-half times longer than our own Earth year. It means that Vesta is moving through space at about 12 mi. (20 km) per second.

Vesta also spins, or rotates, quite fast for an asteroid, once every 5 hours 20 minutes. This time is the "day" for an asteroid, compared to Earth's day of 24 hours. If you were on Vesta, you would see the Sun rise, then set, then rise again, all within 5 hours and 20 minutes.

Asteroid families

Certain groups of asteroids orbit close together in clumps. These are known as asteroid families, or Hirayama families, named after the Japanese astronomer, Kiyotsugu Hirayama, who identified the first main families in 1918. Each family is probably the result of a collision in the past, when one large asteroid broke into pieces or fragments. This also explains the irregular, lumpy nature of many smaller asteroids.

Away from the Main Belt

Hundreds of asteroids orbit the Sun but are not in the Main Belt. The Eureka asteroid group circles the Sun along the orbit of Mars, mostly following behind the planet. The first of them, Eureka itself, was discovered in 1990. An asteroid that shares the same orbit as a planet is called a *Trojan asteroid*, so the asteroids in the Eureka group are known as the Mars Trojans. There are also Trojans in the orbit of Jupiter (see panel), as well as Neptune Trojans.

Space Facts

Orbiting asteroids

● Many hundreds of asteroids orbit the Sun along the same path as the planet Jupiter. They are called the Jupiter, or Jovian, Trojans.

● They are in two main groups, one in front of the planet and one behind it.

● Each group is 60 degrees, or one-sixth of a circle, away from Jupiter. These sites are places where the gravities of Jupiter and the Sun balance each other.

● Discoveries in 2006 show that some of the Jupiter Trojans may be captured comets instead of asteroids.

Asteroids like Antiope are binary, which means there are two rocky objects orbiting the Sun, and twirling around each other at the same time.

Asteroids near Earth

Numerous asteroids orbit the Sun close to our home world, Earth. We can study these asteroids in more detail and even visit them with spacecraft—but they also present the threat of collision with our planet.

Close to home

The general name for asteroids that go around the Sun in orbits close to Earth's orbit is *Near-Earth Asteroids (NEAs)*. One group is the Amors. The asteroids in this group circle the Sun just outside the orbit of our home planet. They do not actually cross our orbital path, although some cross the orbit of the next planet outward, Mars.

One Amor asteroid is Eros, which was visited by the *NEAR-Shoemaker* spacecraft from 2000 to 2001 (see page 23).

It is possible that the two tiny moons of Mars, Phobos and Deimos, were asteroids that have been "captured" by the gravity of Mars. It is also possible that some NEAs are burned-out or extinct comets.

These computer-colored views show Eros from different angles, as it rolls and tumbles through space.

Earth-crossers

The Amors do not pose a collision threat to Earth. But some NEAs do. These are asteroids whose orbits do cross our own planet's orbit, and they are known as Earth-crossers, or *Earth-Crossing Objects (ECOs)*. There are two main groups of ECOs, the Atens and Apollos.

Why ECOs cross Earth's orbit

How can these asteroids cross Earth's orbit if they are going around the Sun like our planet? The orbits of planets and asteroids around the Sun are not perfect circles, but oval-like "squashed circles" called *ellipses*. The Atens are mostly just inside Earth's orbit, but at the farthest point in their ellipses, they cross to the outside of it. The Apollos are the opposite. They are usually outside Earth's orbit, but at the narrowest part of the ellipse they cross to the inside.

How do we know?

The fat banana

The first spacecraft dedicated to studying an asteroid was *NEAR-Shoemaker*. It reached Eros in 2000 and went into orbit around it. The probe's information and pictures showed that Eros was shaped like a "fat banana" about 20 miles (33 kilometers) long, with a deep gouge on one side and a large crater on the other.

The NEAR-Shoemaker probe finally landed on asteroid Eros on February 12, 2001.

Collision with Earth?

If some asteroids have orbits that cross the orbit of Earth, could one smash into our planet at some time? If so, what would be the result? That depends...

What are the chances?

There are many estimates for the chance of an asteroid crashing into Earth. All are very remote, usually many billions to one. But given the immense time spans involved, over billions of years, a collision has almost certainly occurred in the past, and another is likely in the future. In 1989, there was a "near-miss" as asteroid Asclepius passed 434,000 mi. (700,000 km) away (in terms of the vast distances of space, that is very near). In 2004, the smaller 2004 FH, about 98 feet (30 meters) across, came within 26,600 mi. (43,000 km)—eight times closer than the Moon.

In the movie Deep Impact, one part of a comet hits Earth and causes some damage. A smallish asteroid impact would have a similar effect, but a big asteroid would be truly devastating.

Space Fact

A possible collision

● In 2004, scientists worked out that asteroid 2004 MN4 (99942 Apophis) could crash into Earth in the year 2029. Further study showed that this was unlikely. But a collision is still possible farther into the future, in 2036 or 2068.

An asteroid heading for Earth would start to heat up and glow as it entered the atmosphere (layer of air).

Impact disaster

If there is a collision, what happens depends on the size and speed of the asteroid, where it strikes Earth (land or sea, desert or mountains), and the angle of the impact. Any asteroid more than half a mile across would probably cause global disaster. It would set off huge earthquakes and tsunamis (giant waves). It could throw dust or water droplets into the air that would blot out the Sun for months or years, leading to global cooling and plants withering in the gloom. Animals and people would then run out of food. It could be the end of human civilization as we know it.

Saving Earth

Many organizations keep watch for asteroids and other space objects approaching Earth (see page 39). If an asteroid appears to be on a collision course with Earth, what could we do? One possibility is to launch rockets equipped with nuclear explosives. These could blow up near the asteroid and knock it onto a different course, or even land on the asteroid and explode to crack it into pieces.

How do we know?

Asteroid damage on Earth

An asteroid collision may have wiped out the dinosaurs and many other animals and plants 65 million years ago. Rocks formed at this time on Earth contain unusually large amounts of the metal iridium. Iridium is rare on Earth, but common in asteroids. Scientists suggest that an asteroid 6 miles (10 kilometers) wide smashed into what is now the sea off the Yucatan region of Mexico, blowing apart into billions of fragments that eventually settled on the ground and formed an iridium-rich layer of rock. A huge dip called the Chicxulub Crater under the seabed mud may be the site of the asteroid's impact.

25

Bodies Beyond Neptune

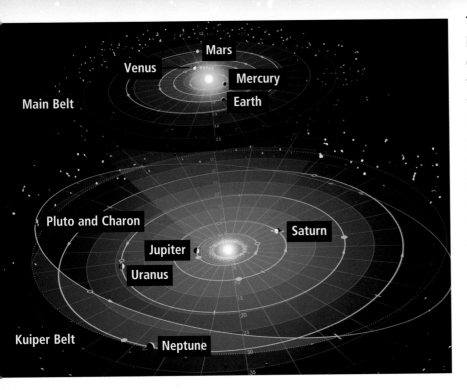

Main Belt

Mars

Venus

Mercury

Earth

Pluto and Charon

Saturn

Jupiter

Uranus

Kuiper Belt

Neptune

In the whole Solar System, the Sun and four inner planets are relatively close (central area, enlarged in gold). The four outer planets (blue) are much farther apart. The Kuiper Belt, with the dwarf planets Pluto and Charon (far left), is beyond Neptune (lower left).

The huge planet Neptune is the eighth planet of our Solar System—30 times farther away from the Sun than Earth. Beyond Neptune is an area of the Solar System that is now being studied in more detail with the latest powerful telescopes and more advanced spacecraft.

The Kuiper Belt

Neptune is the outermost of the giant planets and its pull of gravity, interacting with the Sun's gravity, keeps various objects out there on the fringes of the Solar System, orbiting the Sun. The mysterious zone beyond Neptune is known as the Kuiper Belt. It is named after Gerard Kuiper, the astronomer who first suggested its existence in 1950–51. The Belt probably finishes more than 4,340 million miles (7,000 million kilometers) from the Sun, which is about 45–50 times greater than the Earth-Sun distance.

Objects in the Kuiper Belt and beyond

There are thought to be huge numbers of objects in the Kuiper Belt that resemble asteroids, comets, planets, and similar bodies. They have the general name of *Kuiper Belt Objects (KBOs)*. Another name is *Trans-Neptunian Objects (TNOs)*, which includes not only the objects in the Kuiper Belt but any that may be beyond it. Astronomers think there may be an even bigger doughnut-shaped zone of objects next to the Kuiper Belt, known as the Scattered Disk, which is probably outside what we regard as the Solar System.

Groups of KBOs

The first object classed as a KBO was asteroidlike and discovered in 1992. Its official name is 15760 1992 QB1 but it is usually just called "QB1," or "cubewan." It has given its name to one group of KBOs, the cubewanos. Other types include the plutinos ("little Plutos"), which have features similar to Pluto, the former ninth planet of the Solar System.

No longer a planet

Pluto was discovered in 1930, and its relatively large moon, Charon, was found in 1978. In 2006, the International Astronomical Union decided that there should be eight planets, stopping at Neptune. Both Pluto and Charon were put into a new group called the "dwarf planets." (The largest asteroid, Ceres, was also included as a "dwarf planet.")

An object larger than Pluto was found in the Kuiper Belt in 2003. Known as 2003 UB313, it has been named Eris. Hailed as the "tenth planet" when it was discovered in 2006, it, too, was grouped with Pluto, Charon, and Ceres as a "dwarf planet." Doubtless in the years to come, many similar KBOs will join the "dwarf planet" list.

The deep-space probe New Horizons, launched in 2006, is due to visit Pluto, Charon, and other KBOs from 2015 onward.

Space Facts

The Kuiper Belt

● The inner edge of the Kuiper Belt is near the orbit of Neptune, almost 2,790 million mi. (4,500 million km) from the Sun. The outer edge may extend more than 4,340 million mi. (7,000 million km) from the Sun.

● The "dwarf planet" Pluto's orbit is so "squashed" into an ellipse that at its closest to the Sun, it is 2,750 million mi. (4,435 million km), and at its farthest, 4,526 million mi. (7,300 million km). This means Pluto crosses from the inside to the outside of the Kuiper Belt twice during each orbit.

The Three "M's

Three terms beginning with "m" are often confused. These are meteoroid, meteor, and meteorite. One is found in space, the second in Earth's atmosphere, and the third here on the ground.

Meteors are best seen at night, but sometimes they show up at dawn or dusk.

Meteoroid

A *meteoroid* is a little lump or piece of rock in space, usually much smaller than an asteroid—it ranges in size from a few yards across down to the size of a grain of sand or tinier. Meteoroids may have wandering, random, or haphazard paths through space, instead of going around the Sun in regular orbits. Most meteoroids are fragments of asteroids, comets, moons, and other bodies that have been broken apart by collisions.

Meteor

A *meteor* is the streak of light that is formed as a meteoroid "burns up" when it enters Earth's atmosphere. It is often called a "falling star" or "shooting star." Meteors occur high in the atmosphere, usually above 31 mi. (50 km), which is high above the clouds, and much higher than the typical cruising height of jet aircraft at around 6–7 mi. (10–12 km).

How do we know?
Meteorite strikes

Through telescopes we can see impact craters caused by meteorite strikes on other planets, moons, and asteroids. In 2005, the wheeled, robotlike rover *Opportunity* on Mars found a piece of rock there about the size of a basketball. This has been named the Meridiani Planum meteorite (see opposite).

Meteorite

Most meteoroids burn up completely as meteors. But some are very large, or resistant to melting, or strike the atmosphere at a certain angle. They are not totally burned away. One or more pieces survive and fall to the Earth's surface. These are called *meteorites*. In fact, meteorites fall not only onto Earth, but onto other space objects, too, including other planets, moons, and asteroids. For example, many craters can be clearly seen on Mars and on Earth's Moon. These craters were made by meteorite impacts.

The Mars meteorite photographed by the Opportunity rover in January 2005, and nicknamed "SpongeBob," is an iron-nickel meteorite.

Space Facts

Danger!

● Meteoroids are a constant danger to spacecraft, including satellites and long-distance space probes.

● When astronauts go on "space walks," they wear spacesuits that are specifically designed to resist micrometeoroids. These are very small particles, smaller than a pinhead, that might otherwise puncture the suit and let the air leak out.

● One spacecraft in orbit for four years was struck by at least 79 micrometeoroids. The largest measured about 0.002 inch (50 micrometers) across—about the width of a human hair.

Shooting Stars

Space Facts

Displays from debris

- Some meteors are caused not by natural objects from space, but by artificial items made by people. These may be parts of old rockets, spacecraft, and satellites that have been in Earth's orbit but gradually arc down into the atmosphere.

- A spectacular display of meteors occurred when parts of the old *Mir* space station fell back to Earth in March 2001.

A sudden streak of light in the clear night sky is often called a "shooting star" or "falling star." It is not a star at all, but a tiny piece of rock, a meteoroid, ending its immense journey through space as it burns up in Earth's atmosphere.

Heat and light

The "shooting star" trail, or streak of light, is a meteor. As a meteoroid zooms into the thickening layer of air around Earth, it rubs against the air particles (atoms and molecules). It also squashes the air particles in front of it by a process known as *ram pressure*. The rubbing or friction of air resistance and the ram pressure generate so much heat that the air begins to glow, and the meteoroid itself melts and turns to vapor. The light generated shows as a fast-moving streak across the dark sky.

Meteors at great heights can be photographed through telescopes.

As a rocky meteoroid approaches Earth and burns up in the thickening atmosphere, it leaves a trail of light called a meteor.

Millions every day

Millions of tiny meteoroids fall toward Earth every 24 hours as the planet races through space. They arrive at speeds of up to 43 miles (70 kilometers) per second. Those that come in daylight cannot be seen forming meteors, because the Sun is too bright. On clear nights, the smallest burn up so high in the atmosphere (62 mi. or 100 km) that their glow is not visible from the ground. Slightly larger ones, about the size of the dot on this "i," make it farther down into the atmosphere, but usually burn up by 31 mi. (50 km) high.

The fate of larger meteoroids depends on how fast they travel, the angle at which they meet Earth's atmosphere, and their chemical makeup (see page 35). Some cause much brighter glows or trails and may heat up so quickly that they burn as fast as "fireballs," or even explode in a bright flash, known as a *bolide*.

Space Fact

Light trails

● The length of a meteoroid's light trail and how long it lasts depend on the meteoroid's size and chemical makeup. Small, fast-moving particles form light trails that last just a few seconds, but larger meteoroids can produce a glow that lasts for half an hour or more.

Meteor Showers and Storms

A meteor happens an average of every few seconds somewhere around Earth. But at certain times they become much more common, and the clear night sky seems alive with streaks and flashes. These are meteor showers. If there are even more light trails, they are meteor storms.

Long ago, people often linked meteor showers—along with eclipses and comets—to the anger of gods or the wrath of spirits. By the 1900s, scientists had worked out why meteors sometimes come in showers or storms. The usual reason is that Earth, on its long orbit around the Sun, is passing through tiny bits of dust and debris left by a long-gone comet. These remnants "hang" like a dusty streamer in space, tracing the comet's orbit. Each time Earth comes around, it encounters some of the particles.

Yearly showers

Because Earth orbits the Sun once each year, these meteor showers occur at predictable times of the year. For example, the Perseid shower is usually around August 11–12 (see panel on page 33). It is caused by dust and debris from a comet that passed in 1862. The Eta Aquarids in May and the Orionids in October happen when Earth passes through the debris, or orbital dust cloud, left by Halley's Comet.

This photograph of the Leonid shower, taken over many minutes, shows ordinary stars moving as slightly curved streaks. The meteors seem to burst out from one area called the radiant (middle right).

Parallel movement

Imagine looking down a multilane highway into the distance. The vehicles are moving parallel to each other. But to the viewer, they seem to come from one distant spot and get farther apart as they come closer. In the same way, the streaks of light in a meteor shower seem to "explode" from one place in the sky. In fact, they are also moving parallel to each other. The spot where they seem to originate is known as the *radiant*. The constellation (pattern of stars) where the radiant lies gives its name to the meteor shower. The Perseid shower originates from Perseus. The Leonid shower, due to the comet Tempel-Tuttle (see page 10), originates from Leo. (Perseus is almost overhead at about 10 p.m. in North America and Europe in January, and Leo is down near the horizon looking east at the same time and place.)

The Moon has no atmosphere, so when a meteoroid crashes there, it does not slow down or leave a trail of light.

Night spectacle

Meteor showers and storms make a spectacular sight, and people gather at popular viewing points away from city lights to admire the display. During a typical shower, there are between 5 and 60 meteors every hour—that is, up to one each minute. But some heavy showers or storms peak at one meteor every second. The meteor "downpours" can affect radio, television, and long-distance communications by producing bursts of energy high in the atmosphere.

SPACE DATA

Some main meteor showers:

Name of shower	Date of peak
Quadrantids	3 January
Eta Aquarids	4 May
Delta Aquarids	29 July
Perseids	11–12 August
Orionids	20–21 October
Leonids	16–17 November
Geminids	13 December

Crashing into Earth

Only a tiny fraction of meteoroids survive their journey through Earth's atmosphere and reach the surface as meteorites. Rarely, a large meteorite smashes into the ground and causes great damage. But most meteorite impacts are small and go unnoticed.

Space Facts

Landing on Earth

- Scientists estimate that between 200 and 1,000 tons of meteoroid material lands on Earth's surface each day.

- In one year about 500 meteorites reach the surface. Some are as small as peas, while very rarely (once every year or two) there is one bigger than a person. However of these 500, most fall in the sea or on remote areas of land.

- Only five or so meteorites yearly may be actually noticed and recorded by people.

Falling speed

As meteorites fall through the thickening atmosphere, increasing air resistance makes them move slower and slower. They slow down when they reach Earth's atmosphere and end up simply "falling" at a speed where the pull of Earth's gravity bringing them down is balanced by the air's resistance to their movement. Their impact speed is about 330–490 feet (100–150 meters) per second—four times faster than a car on the highway.

A piece of one of the largest meteorites ever found on Earth is displayed at the American Museum of Natural History in New York City, NY.

Larger meteorites, usually those that contain plenty of iron, may have enough mass to keep some of the speed they had in space, and so they hit the ground harder. This applies even more to asteroids, which are even bigger. The impact speed of even a small asteroid could be up to 32,800 feet (10,000 meters) per second, and a larger one is twice as fast.

The effect of a meteorite impact (see page 36) depends not only on its size and speed, but also on the angle it strikes the ground, and the nature of the ground. Soft soil or mud soaks up the energy of the impact, so there are few lasting effects.

A magnified view of a meteorite shows tiny, colorful lumps of minerals, mostly up to 0.04 inch (1 millimeter) across.

Types of meteorites

For many years, meteorites have been put in one of three groups:

- Stony (rocky) with silicate minerals.

- Iron (metallic), usually mixed iron and nickel, with about nine-tenths iron.

- Mixed, with both stony minerals and iron-based metals.

Newer ways of grouping them depend on their more detailed chemical makeup and whether or not they contain tiny, ball-shaped lumps of minerals known as *chondrules*. Those that have chondrules are known as *chondrites*, and those without are *achondrites*. Studying the makeup of meteorites helps scientists to understand the objects that they came from, such as asteroids or comets.

Great Meteorite Strikes

Once every million years or so, Earth is probably hit by a small asteroid or large meteorite, which has global effects. Smaller meteorite impacts are more common, perhaps leaving a crater several hundred meters across. But over time Earth's wind, rain, and weather wear away the rocks. Plants grow and soil, sand, or mud collect. So gradually the signs of these impact craters disappear.

Classic crater

One of the most striking and well-shaped impact craters is the Barringer or Meteor Crater (Canyon Diablo Crater) near Winslow, Arizona. It is about 4,132 feet (1,260 meters) across, 590 feet (180 meters) deep, and surrounded by a rim 148 feet (45 meters) high. It was probably formed about 50,000 years ago by a meteorite about 164 feet (50 meters) across that weighed up to 330,000 tons, which exploded when it hit the ground. The crater left by the impact has been preserved so well because of the dry desert conditions.

A mysterious explosion

In 1908, a huge explosion shook the region of Tunguska, Siberia. No crater was formed. But the damage was huge, with trees blasted and other shock-wave damage over an area of 1,544 square mi. (4,000 square km). One explanation is that a meteorite (or perhaps a piece of comet) about 98 feet (30 meters) across exploded at a height of 6 mi. (10 km) as it hurtled down at a 45-degree angle.

One of the biggest, best-preserved meteorite craters is the Barringer Crater in Arizona.

Space Facts

A meteorite from Mars

● In 1996, scientists studying a meteorite from Antarctica decided that it had come from Mars. It was perhaps knocked off the planet's surface by another meteorite strike.

● Known as ALH84001, the Martian meteorite apparently had microscopic wormlike "fossils" in it. This suggested that Mars supported some form of life long ago.

● However, other scientists claim that the "fossils" are simply natural formations of minerals in the rock.

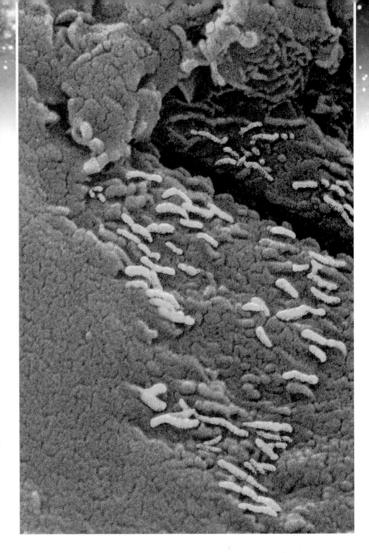

The "fossils" in Mars meteorite ALH84001 could be remains of microscopic life forms, like bacteria on Earth.

Famous meteorites

The biggest known meteorite on Earth is the Hoba meteorite of Namibia (see panel). The Willamette meteorite first studied by scientists in Oregon in 1902 is about 10 feet (3 meters) long and weighs 14.4 tons. The Cape York meteorite from Greenland's west coast, discovered in 1897, weighs almost 34 tons and was taken to New York City for display.

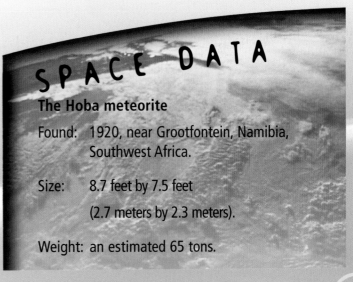

SPACE DATA

The Hoba meteorite

Found: 1920, near Grootfontein, Namibia, Southwest Africa.

Size: 8.7 feet by 7.5 feet (2.7 meters by 2.3 meters).

Weight: an estimated 65 tons.

How we Observe Comets, Asteroids, and Meteors

Compared to looking at planets such as Jupiter and Saturn, searching for small space bodies like comets and asteroids is difficult and ruled by luck. But new telescopes and spacecraft, as well as more powerful computers, are discovering more small space objects at a steadily increasing rate.

Keeping watch

The lone amateur studying the night sky still has a chance of finding a comet or asteroid, or noticing a new meteor shower. But today's professional astronomers belong to big organizations involved in the lookout for new asteroids, comets, and similar objects. In particular, "asteroid-watching" has become an exciting business, since one day an asteroid could be spotted that is on a collision course with Earth. The people who find it will then become the focus for world attention and saving our planet because they will have alerted everyone to the approaching danger.

The telescope-housing domes and buildings nicknamed "Science City" on Maui, Hawaii, are part of the NEAT asteroid-watching system.

How do we know?

Testing radioactivity

Rocks and fossils on Earth are tested in various ways to show when they formed. These tests include detecting the amount of radiation energy—radioactivity—the rocks contain. Meteorites can be tested in the same way to find their age. Comets and asteroids can also be tested, by spacecraft that land on them or collect their dust and fragments from space. Some meteorites, comets, and bits of asteroids have been dated at billions of years old. They give clues to the nature of rocky objects in space soon after the Solar System formed. One of the oldest is the Krahenberg meteorite, which could go back more than 4,500 million years almost to the "birth" of the Solar System.

The Kitt Peak National Observatory in Arizona has more than 20 telescopes, which have discovered many hundreds of comets and asteroids.

For their space surveys, professional astronomers use massively powerful telescopes that automatically scan the sky, taking thousands of pictures every night. Most are wide-field optical telescopes that see a large part of the sky, rather than a highly magnified tiny part.

Computer-powered searches

Pictures are taken through the telescopes by digital cameras and fed into supercomputers. These automatically compare the pictures with each other and with pictures in the memory banks, to find objects that are new or moving in an unusual way. Using this method, thousands of asteroids are discovered every month. The results are coordinated by several organizations, such as NASA, the U.S. National Aeronautics and Space Administration, and Spaceguard (see panel). They share sky-scanning, so that as much of space as possible is viewed each night.

Space Facts

Asteroid-watchers

● LINEAR, the Lincoln Near-Earth Asteroid Research program, has its base near Socorro, New Mexico.

● LONEOS, the Lowell Observatory Near-Earth Object Search, is also looking for Earth-crossing asteroids and comets. It is based at the Lowell Observatory near Flagstaff, Arizona.

● NEAT, the Near-Earth Asteroid Tracking setup, is organized by NASA's JPL (Jet Propulsion Laboratory) in Pasadena, California. It has two main telescope locations at the Maui Space Surveillance Site on the island of Maui, Hawaii, and the Palomar Observatory in California.

● Spacewatch is based at the University of Arizona's Lunar and Planetary Laboratory in Tucson, Arizona.

● CINEOS, the Campo Imperatore Near-Earth Object Survey, has its headquarters at the Rome Observatory, Italy.

● Spaceguard is an international group working with bodies such as the European Space Agency, the United Nations, and the organizations listed here. It has telescopes in many countries, including Japan, Australia, and the U.K.

How we Explore Comets, Asteroids, and Meteors

Many space probes have headed out into deep space to fly past or land on comets, asteroids, and other small space objects. Some take "normal" photographs using light. Others use radio waves to detect size and shape, or pick up rays and waves from the object, such as infrared (heat) rays and even X-rays. All of this information is changed into radio waves to send back to Earth.

Meeting comets

The first deep-space craft to fly past a comet was *ICE*, the *International Cometary Explorer*. After its launch in 1978, it went close to Comet Giacobini-Zinner in 1985, on its way to Halley's Comet in 1986. Halley's Comet was also viewed by other craft, including *Giotto* (see page 9). Other comet-visiting craft are *Stardust*, which flew past asteroid Annefrank and close to Comet Wild 2, *Deep Space 1* (launched in 1998), *Rosetta* (2004), and *Deep Impact* (2005).

Another probe, *CONTOUR* (*Comet Nucleus Tour*) was launched in 2002 with the aim of visiting the Comets Encke in 2003, Schwassmann-Wachmann 3 in 2006, and d'Arrest in 2008. Sadly, contact with it was lost when it boosted out of Earth orbit.

Deep Impact's "lander" or impactor, smashed into Comet Tempel 1 at an incredible speed of 32,800 ft. (10,000 m) per second.

Asteroid visits

In 1991, the far-traveling *Galileo* probe traveled past the asteroids Gaspra and Ida, on its way to the giant planet Jupiter. It discovered the first moon orbiting an asteroid when it detected Dactyl going around Ida.

NASA's car-sized *NEAR-Shoemaker* (*Near-Earth Asteroid Rendezvous*, see pages 22-23) set off in 1996. It passed by the Main Belt asteroid Mathilde the following year, taking pictures that showed it was one of the blackest objects ever seen in space.

In November 2005, the Hayabusa craft landed briefly on the small asteroid Itokawa, which is only about feet 1,770 ft. (540 m) long.

Space Facts

Sending probes into deep space

● *Deep Space 1*, launched in 1998, went past the asteroid Braille at a distance of only 16 miles (26 kilometers) in 1999.

● It traveled past Comet Wilson-Harrington in 2001. Later that year, it passed within 1,365 mi. (2,200 km) of Comet Borrelly.

● In 2003, the Japanese *Hayabusa* probe was launched toward asteroid Itokawa. The plan was to arrive there in 2005, land, and collect samples of the surface to bring back to Earth. The craft has suffered several problems, but it is hoped that it will eventually return to Earth.

After several problems, *NEAR-Shoemaker* made a "swingby" pass back near Earth, so that it could use Earth's gravity to redirect its course, approaching to just 335 mi. (540 km). It then headed off again to orbit around the near-Earth asteroid Eros in 2000. It landed on the surface of Eros in 2001 and sent back 69 close-up pictures. Finally, two weeks after landing the probe was shut down. Like other landers on similar space objects, it is still there.

The Future

Over the coming years, telescopes will continue to scan the skies for exciting new comets, spectacular meteor showers, and the worrying threat of a suddenly-detected asteroid heading for our world. Also, several space probes are planned for launch, to visit small objects in deep space.

In 2005, Rosetta came within 930 miles (1,500 kilometers) of Earth on a "flyby," before heading out to encounter asteroids and comets.

Current and future missions

The European Space Agency's *Rosetta* space probe was launched in 2004. The first part of its mission is to study the Main Belt asteroids Steins in 2008 and Lutetia in 2010. Then, after "hibernating" to save energy for three years, it is due to meet Comet Churyumov-Gerasimenko in 2014. A lander called *Philae* will touch down softly on the comet's surface, as the main probe orbits and then follows the comet's path. Together they will monitor the deep-frozen comet as it heads toward the Sun, warms up, "switches on," and loops around the Sun in 2015.

The NASA space agency's *Dawn* mission in 2007 is to the Main Belt. It should orbit the large asteroid, Vesta, in 2011, then the "dwarf planet" Ceres (formerly seen as the biggest asteroid) in 2015.

Looking out

The coming years will see continued space surveys and asteroid-watching for any object that is likely to threaten planet Earth. There will also be new comets, unpredictably appearing as if from nowhere. Far into the future, it may be possible to send craft to asteroids and meteorites, to mine their metals and minerals that are very rare on Earth, and return these valuable resources to our home planet.

New Horizons

One of the most ambitious and the most complex of all space probes is *New Horizons*. It left Earth in 2006 on an immense journey to Pluto and then the Kuiper Belt. In the meantime, telescopes here on Earth will continue to improve and be able to peer out to the distant edge of the Solar System in more detail. Some astronomers expect to discover swarms of exciting new objects in the Kuiper Belt, the Scattered Disk, and beyond. The former view that the Solar System "ended" at the planet Pluto has already changed greatly. Pluto is no longer regarded as a true planet. We also know there are vast numbers of objects beyond it, including comets and various asteroidlike objects— whose numbers may be in the millions, or even billions.

Far into the future, "asteroid mining" to obtain rare and valuable minerals may become possible. But saving Earth's own resources would be much cheaper and less dangerous.

SPACE DATA

The *New Horizons* mission plan:

2006	Launch from Earth
	Fly past Main Belt asteroid JF56
2007	Fly past Jupiter for gravity-assist boost
2015	Visit Pluto and Charon
	Closest approach to Pluto, 6,200 miles (10,000 kilometers)
2016	Continue through Kuiper Belt, locating and studying KBOs
2025	Shutdown

Timeline of Discovery

65 million years ago A massive meteorite or asteroid may have struck Earth, causing a global catastrophe that wiped out the dinosaurs and many other animals and plants.

50,000 years ago The Barringer or Meteor Crater (Canyon Diablo Crater) in Arizona was formed by an impact; it was discovered by scientists in 1871.

1070s Halley's Comet was pictured on the Bayeux Tapestry depicting the Battle of Hastings and the Norman invasion of England in 1066.

1492 The first scientific record of a meteorite fall in modern times was made in Ensisheim, Alsace.

1801 Giuseppe Piazzi observed Ceres, which was first believed to be a planet, then became the first asteroid to be officially discovered, and then in 2006 was "promoted" again to become a dwarf planet.

1802 The second asteroid was discovered, Pallas. Juno followed in 1804 and Vesta in 1807.

1845 The postmaster and amateur astronomer, Karl Hencke, discovered Astraea, the fifth asteroid to be found, almost 40 years after the fourth.

1906 Max Wolf discovered the first of the Trojan asteroids following the same path as planet Jupiter.

1908 A huge explosion in Tunguska, Siberia, caused immense damage; it may have been a meteoroid or piece of comet that exploded several miles above the ground.

Devastation in the aftermath of the explosion in Tunguska, Siberia, in 1908.

1932 The first Earth-crossing asteroid, Apollo, was discovered.

1947 The second-biggest "meteoroidal event" of the twentieh century (after Tunguska) occurred in Sikhote-Alin, Eastern Russia. A meteorite exploded about 3 miles (5 kilometers) high and the largest fragments made small pits and craters.

1950 An astronomer, Fred Whipple, suggested his "dirty snowball" theory for the makeup of a comet.

1950 Jan Oort suggested that comets might come from a gigantic "shell" of objects far beyond the Solar System, now known as the Oort Cloud.

1951 Gerard Kuiper suggested the existence of swarms of objects beyond the planet Neptune, in the zone now called the Kuiper Belt.

1986 Halley's Comet came near Earth; its next visit is in 2061.

1994 Parts of Comet Shoemaker-Levy 9 plunged into the giant planet Jupiter.

The New Horizons probe.

1998 The *Deep Space 1* craft was launched and traveled past three comets in three years.

2001 *NEAR-Shoemaker* spacecraft visited the near-Earth asteroid Eros and showed it looked like a "fat banana."

2004 The *Stardust* space probe passed by Comet Wild 2 and collected samples of its coma.

2004 The *Rosetta* space probe set off to meet asteroids in the Main Belt in 2008 and 2010, then Comet Churyumov-Gerasimenko in 2014.

2005 A small "impactor" from spacecraft *Deep Impact* smashed into the surface of the nucleus of Comet Tempel 1.

2006 The *New Horizons* probe set off to the edge of the Solar System, on a 20-year mission to visit Pluto and other objects in the Kuiper Belt.

Glossary

asteroid A rocky object that orbits the Sun, but that is not large enough to be a planet.

astronomer A scientist who specializes in the study of space.

chondrules Tiny ball-like, glassy lumps of minerals, usually rich in silica, found in certain kinds of meteorites.

coma In a comet, the glow that surrounds the core or nucleus of the head region.

comet A small, icy object that comes near to the Sun.

crater A dish-shaped hole in the surface of a planet, moon, or other space object.

ECO Earth-Crossing Object, a space object, such as an asteroid, that crosses the path of Earth's orbit.

gravity A pulling or attracting force possessed by all objects, mass, and matter.

Kuiper Belt A ringlike area of the Solar System beyond the planet Neptune, but not as far out as the Oort Cloud.

Main Belt Another name for the Asteroid Belt between Mars and Jupiter, where most asteroids are found.

mass Matter, or substance, in terms of the numbers and types of atoms or other tiny particles.

meteor A streak or flash of light, often called a "shooting star" or "falling star," caused by a meteoroid burning up as it enters Earth's atmosphere.

meteor shower Many meteors that occur close together.

meteorite A small, usually rocky particle from space that crashes onto the surface of a planet, moon, or other space body.

meteoroid A piece of rock, metal, or similar substance, smaller than an asteroid, that moves through space.

NEA Near-Earth Asteroid, an asteroid that orbits relatively close to our planet.

nonperiodic comet A comet that passes the Sun once and heads away into deep space.

nucleus In a comet, the small, rocky centre or core inside the "head."

observatory (astronomical observatory) A building or place, usually with telescopes and similar equipment, where people study objects in space.

Oort Cloud An immense ball-like "shell" of space objects, including perhaps billions of comets, that surrounds the Solar System at a vast distance.

orbit The path of one object going around another, such as a planet around the Sun, or a moon around a planet.

periodic comet A comet that goes around, or orbits, the Sun on a regular journey.

probe A spacecraft launched into space to send back information about objects such as asteroids and comets.

radiant The place in the sky from which the meteors in a meteor shower all seem to come from.

radiation Energy that spreads out or radiates from its source, often in the form of rays or waves.

Scattered Disk A doughnut-shaped region of space beyond the Kuiper Belt, where many objects may occur.

tail In a comet, a long stream of gas or dust that points away from the Sun (rather than trailing behind the comet).

Trojan asteroid An asteroid that follows the same path or orbit as a planet.

Further Information

Books

Asteroids, Comets and Meteors (Worlds Beyond), Ron Miller (21st Century, 2004)

Discovering Comets and Meteors (Isaac Asimov's New Library of the Universe), Isaac Asimov (Gareth Stevens Publishing, 1996)

National Geographic Encyclopedia of Space, Linda K Glover (National Geographic, 2004)

Organizations

National Aeronautics & Space Administration (NASA)
Organization that runs the space program
www.nasa.gov

International Astronomical Union (IAU)
The official world astronomy organization, responsible for naming stars, planets, moons, and other objects in space
www.iau.org

International Meteor Organization
Produces calendars and advice on meteors, showers, and storms, and the scientific journal WGN
www.imo.net/

Spaceguard
Dedicated to keeping watch for asteroids, comets, and other space objects that could be a threat to Earth
spaceguard.esa.int/

Jet Propulsion Laboratory (JPL)
Center responsible for NASA's robot space probes
www.jpl.nasa.gov

European Space Agency (ESA)
Organization responsible for space flight and exploration by European countries
www.esa.int

The Planetary Society
Organization devoted to the exploration of the Solar System
www.planetary.org

Web sites

Due to the changing nature of Internet links, The Rosen Publishing Group, Inc., has developed an online list of Web sites related to the subject of this book. This site is updated regularly. Please use this link to access the list:
www.rosenlinks.com/eas/comets/

Index

Numbers in **bold** indicate pictures.

ML

9/07